BLOOM

Olympiad ACE

A Comprehensive Practice Book

for School Olympiads & Talent Search Exams

ENGLISH

Class 2

by
Dolly Jain

Olympiad ACE

BLOOM
Bloom Cap Edu Ventures Pvt. Ltd.

Administrative & Production Office
'Ramchhaya' 4577/15, Agarwal Road, Darya Ganj, New Delhi -110002
Tele: 011- 47630600, 43518550

PRICE: ₹125.00

PO No. : TXT-59-T067186-09-25

Published by Arihant Publications (I) Ltd.

For further information about the books log on to
www.bloomcap.org

Follow us on

Preface

"Future belongs to those Who prepares for it today"

School Olympiads are National & International level competitions conducted by different Government, Non-Government & Educational Organisations with the purpose of making the children ready to face competitive exams.

The challenging Questions asked in Olympiads motivate them to learn more & more and bring out the best results with improved academic performance. The Awards & Scholarship offered by Olympiads motivate children to aspire & strive for doing better and emerge out to be the best.

English Olympiads

English is one of the most widely spoken languages across the world. In today's era, good command over English is considered as a must have skill. The greatest advantage of studying English is improvement in communication skills along with the growth of personality.

English Olympiads are meant to strengthen students' command over this universal language by improving spellings, grammar, sentence structure and to master student's language skills.

'Bloom English Olympiad Study Book Class 2' is a perfect resource to Study & Practice for Olympiad Exams and other National & State Level Talent Search Exams & Other Competitions.

Some Special Features of Bloom English Olympiad Study Books are;

- Complete coverage of all the aspects of English; Grammar, Reading Comprehension, Writing Skills, Spellings, Vocabulary & Communication Skills.
- Chapterwise Exercises having different types of Objective Questions at par with the Olympiad Level.
- Olympiad Pattern Practice Sets at the end.

This book is prepared by Expert Panel with the utmost care, still if you have any suggestions regarding its improvement then feel free to contact us at support@bloomcap.org. We will try to inculcate your suggestions in the further editions.

Contents

Chapter 01

Nouns

Directions (Q. Nos. 1-5) Find out the noun from the given sentences.

1. We worship God daily.
(a) We (b) worship
(c) God (d) daily

2. The mother loves us the most.
(a) The (b) mother
(c) us (d) most

3. He comes from Kanyakumari.
(a) He (b) comes
(c) from (d) Kanyakumari

4. Our team has won the match.
(a) team
(b) match
(c) Both (a) and (b)
(d) None of the above

5. Rajeev played guitar in the function.
(a) Rajeev (b) guitar
(c) function (d) All of these

Directions (Q. Nos. 6-8) Select the proper noun from the given words.

6. (a) Paris (b) Country
(c) Capital (d) City

7. (a) Gate
(b) India Gate
(c) Indian
(d) None of the above

8. (a) Player (b) Game
(c) Sport (d) Sania Mirza

Directions (Q. Nos. 9-11) Select the common noun from the given words.

9. (a) Book (b) English
(c) Champak (d) India

10. (a) Diwali (b) Bihu
(c) Festival (d) Christmas

11. (a) Ganga (b) River
(c) Yamuna (d) Nile

Directions (Q. Nos. 12-14) Select the collective noun from the given words.

12. (a) Thief (b) Robber
(c) People (d) Gang

13. (a) Crowd (b) Person
(c) Man (d) Woman

14. (a) Student (b) Class
(c) Teacher (d) Principal

Directions (Q. Nos. 15-17) Select the countable noun from the given words.

15. (a) Tea (b) Coffee
(c) Cup (d) Milk

16. (a) Paper (b) Sugar (c) Plastic (d) Water

17. (a) Bread (b) Butter
(c) Soda (d) Salt

Directions (Q. Nos. 18-20) Identify the uncountable noun from the given words.

18. (a) Watch (b) Time (c) Clock (d) Mobile

19. (a) Musician (b) Singer (c) Guitar (d) Music

20. (a) Stove (b) Salt (c) Ball (d) Basket

Directions (Q. Nos. 21-24) Fill in the blanks with suitable nouns.

21. You must see a .... because of your cold.

(a) teacher (b) doctor (c) hospital (d) engineer

22. This .... comes from tropical forests.

(a) house (b) shadow (c) bottle (d) plant

23. I am very hungry, but the ...... is empty.

(a) wardrobe (b) fridge (c) bucket (d) pool

24. In spite of the ...., he went out.

(a) snow (b) fire (c) earth (d) cool

Directions (Q. Nos. 25-30) Change the singular nouns into the plural nouns.

25. Boy

(a) Boys (b) Boies (c) Either (a) or (b) (d) Neither (a) nor (b)

26. Baby

(a) Babys (b) Babies (c) Either (a) or (b) (d) Neither (a) nor (b)

27. Chair

(a) Chaires (b) Chair (c) Chairs (d) None of these

28. Book

(a) Books (b) Bookses (c) Book (d) All of these

29. Mango

(a) Mangos (b) Mangoos (c) Mangoes (d) None of these

30. Knife

(a) Knives (b) Knifes (c) Knivese (d) Knifs

Directions (Q. Nos. 31-35) Read the passage carefully and answer the questions given below based on nouns.

There is a ...**(31)**... on the ...**(32)**... . The hunters are looking for it. They can't see the bird because it is hiding in the ...**(33)**... The ...**(34)**... is carrying a gun. The small hunter is carrying two ...**(35)**... .

31. (a) hunter (b) bird (c) gun (d) apple

32. (a) tree (b) grass (c) sky (d) land

33. (a) branchs (b) branc (c) branches (d) branchh

34. (a) huntings (b) hunter (c) hunteres (d) huntrs

35. (a) gun (b) stick (c) guns (d) arrows

36. Read the passage and count the number of nouns.

Akshay went to school. He met an old man on the way. The old man was very hungry. So, Akshay gave him his lunch to eat. The old man thanked Akshay a lot.

(a) 3 (b) 2 (c) 5 (d) 1

Chapter 02

Pronouns

Directions (Q. Nos. 1-5) Choose the correct pronoun for the noun given in the brackets.

1. My name is Susan. (Susan) .... am from England.
   (a) She (b) I (c) You (d) It
2. Gaurav and Saurabh are best friends. (Gaurav and Saurabh) .... go to school together.
   (a) We (b) You (c) They (d) Them
3. There is a beautiful house in our colony. (The house) .... has 4 bedrooms.
   (a) She (b) They
   (c) His (d) It
4. My grandparents live in Meerut. (My grand parents) .... often come to see us.
   (a) They (b) You (c) We (d) He
5. Tanya is a little girl but (Tanya) .... sings well.
   (a) he (b) it (c) she (d) you

Directions (Q. Nos. 6-8) Find out pronoun in the sentences given below.

6. Buddy is my pet dog. It likes eggs and chickens.
   (a) my (b) pet
   (c) It (d) All of these
7. Mohit is my neighbour. He studies in my school.
   (a) Mohit (b) He
   (c) my (d) None of these
8. Mansi won the race. She ran very fast.
   (a) very (b) She
   (c) won (d) None of these
9. Match the nouns given in list-I with their pronouns given in List-II.

List I	List II
A. Varun	1. We
B. Shweta and I	2. He
C. Seema, Raju and Rohit	3. She
D. Kirti	4. They

Codes

	A	B	C	D		A	B	C	D
(a)	1	2	3	4	(b)	4	2	1	3
(c)	2	1	4	3	(d)	4	3	2	1

10. Match the following.

List I	List II
A. He	1. Them
B. They	2. Him
C. She	3. Us
D. We	4. Her

Codes

	A	B	C	D		A	B	C	D
(a)	2	1	4	3	(b)	1	2	3	4
(c)	4	3	2	1	(d)	3	4	2	1

Directions (Q. Nos. 11-14) Look at the pictures and answer the questions using pronoun.

11. What is Lucy doing?

.... is reading a book.

(a) He (b) It

(c) They (d) She

12. What is the girl and the boy holding in their hands?

.... are holding mikes in their hands.

(a) He (b) They

(c) She (d) We

13. What is the patient doing in front of a doctor?

.... is showing his tongue.

(a) She (b) They

(c) He (d) It

14. What is the officer holding in his hands?

.... is a kitten.

(a) She (b) It

(c) They (d) He

Directions (Q. Nos. 15-19) Identify the pronoun for the underlined words in the given sentences.

15. <u>John and Peter</u> go to school together.

(a) We (b) They

(c) Us (d) She

16. <u>My mother</u> is a good cook.

(a) He (b) She

(c) It (d) We

17. <u>Zebra</u> has long neck.

(a) We (b) It

(c) He (d) She

18. <u>Harish</u> is a Class III student.

(a) They (b) It

(c) He (d) She

19. <u>My parents, my sister and I</u> are going to Chandigarh.

(a) We (b) They

(c) He (d) It

Directions (Q. Nos. 20-27) Read the passage given below and fill up the blanks with suitable pronouns.

Bheem is an adventurous and fun-loving boy....**(20)**... is 9 years old and has great strength....**(21)**...village's name is Dholakpur. He loves his village and its people....**(22)**... also look foward to Bheem's help in the time of any difficulty. Bheem loves food and sweets specially Ladoo....**(23)**...is his favourite sweet. It gives...**(24)**...energy to fight the enemy. ...**(25)**...friends are Chutki, Jaggu (a monkey) and Raju. ...**(26)**... are always with Bheem to help ...**(27)**.... .

20. (a) He (b) She (c) It (d) I

21. (a) My (b) His (c) Him (d) Our

22. (a) We (b) They (c) He (d) It

23. (a) She (b) They (c) It (d) We

24. (a) his (b) him (c) them (d) us

25. (a) She (b) His (c) Her (d) He

26. (a) They (b) Them (c) We (d) He

27. (a) they (b) him (c) his (d) he

Directions (Q. Nos. 28-30) Read the passage given below and answer the questions from the given options.

Hi! I am a ruler. I help people to draw straight lines. I have markings on me so that people can draw lines of the desired length. Students keep me in their pencil box. I come in different sizes.

28. How many pronouns are used?
(a) 4 (b) 3
(c) 2 (d) 6

29. In the above passage, 'I' stands for
(a) Pencil box (b) People
(c) Students (d) Ruler

30. In the above passage, 'their' stands for
(a) students and ruler
(b) ruler and pencil box
(c) people and students
(d) None of the above

Chapter 03

Verbs

Directions (Q. Nos. 1-10) Fill in the blanks with appropriate verbs to make a meaningful sentence.

1. He .... cartoons on the T.V.

(a) gives (b) runs
(c) watches (d) reads

2. Stars .... in the sky.

(a) twinkle (b) flash
(c) come (d) go

3. The lion .... in the jungle.

(a) barks (b) roars
(c) hoots (d) talks

4. She .... a big car.

(a) runs (b) drives
(c) dislikes (d) travels

5. My mother .... our house everyday.

(a) clean (b) cleans
(c) washes (d) dresses

6. I .... drinking milk.

(a) are (b) have
(c) am (d) is

7. You .... going to school.

(a) was (b) are
(c) am (d) had

8. Students .... sitting in the classroom.

(a) are (b) was
(c) has (d) do

9. A frog .... croaking.

(a) are (b) were
(c) am (d) is

10. They .... not finished their homework.
(a) have (b) has
(c) was (d) did

11. Match the following pronouns given in list-I with helping verbs given in list-II.

List-I		List-II	
A.	We	1.	Am
B.	I	2.	Was
C.	She	3.	Is
D.	It	4.	Are

Codes

	A	B	C	D		A	B	C	D
(a)	1	4	2	3	(b)	3	1	4	2
(c)	4	1	2	3	(d)	2	3	1	4

Directions (Q. Nos. 12-14) Answer the questions based on the given pictures.

12. What is Sumit doing?

Sumit .... on the rope.
(a) is jumping (b) is climbing
(c) are plucking (d) were playing

13. What is Roshni doing?

Roshni .... the book.
(a) is reading (b) were writing
(c) are studying (d) am listening

14. What is Meena doing?

Meena is .... a burger.
(a) cooking (b) preparing
(c) packing (d) eating

Directions (Q.Nos. 15-18) Complete the sentences with the suitable verb.

15. A postman .... the letters.
(a) brings (b) writes
(c) reads (d) picks

16. Doctors .... the patients.
(a) kill (b) punish (c) cure (d) admit

17. A washerman .... clothes.
(a) stiches (b) washes
(c) buys (d) brings

18. Soldiers .... to save their country.
(a) fight (b) kill
(c) murder (d) quarrel

Directions (Q. Nos. 19-24) Read the passage and fill in the blanks with suitable verbs.

There ...**(19)**... a mouse. It could not ...**(20)**... food any where. It ...**(21)**... very thin. At last the mouse ...**(22)**... a basket full of corn. It ...**(23)**... inside through a small hole. It ...**(24)**... a great deal and became very fat. It tried to come out of the basket, but could not as it had become very fat and the hole was very small.

19. (a) is (b) was
(c) lived (d) are

20. (a) get (b) find
(c) eat (d) see

21. (a) grew (b) event
(c) jumped (d) become

22. (a) find (b) found (c) sang (d) show

23. (a) ran (b) slipped
(c) went (d) going

24. (a) drank (b) ate
(c) saw (d) laughed

25. Read the passage and count the number of main/action verbs.

Komal loves singing and dancing. She is eating her lunch right now. After finishing her lunch, she would go to watch a movie with her friend.

(a) 5 (b) 4
(c) 6 (d) 3

Directions (Q.Nos. 26-30) Read the following sentences and choose the one with correct verb in bold.

26. (a) Reshma **eats** an orange everyday.
(b) She **go** to school.
(c) I **are** very hungry.
(d) They **was** walking.

27. (a) Sheena **were** writing a letter.
(b) Children **was** playing outside.
(c) I **carried** the bag myself.
(d) He **throw** the ball.

28. (a) Rohan **tear** the pages.
(b) My mother **cook** good food.
(c) My father **is** a businessman.
(d) He **wear** a red shirt.

29. (a) May I **comes** in?
(b) Why **were** you late today?
(c) Shikha **want** to go outside.
(d) Rahul **were** there yesterday.

30. (a) I do not **know** you.
(b) He **were** exercising.
(c) Please **passed** me that salt!
(d) He **have** a naughty boy.

Chapter 04

Adverbs

Directions (Q. Nos. 1-5) Fill in the blanks with suitable adverbs.

1. The old lady walked .... with the help of a stick.

(a) safely (b) fast
(c) slowly (d) clearly

2. Annie is .... busy over the phone.

(a) sometimes (b) often
(c) seldom (d) always

3. The man though fat, ran ....

(a) fast (b) speedily
(c) continuously (d) fastly

4. The soldiers fought ....

(a) greedily (b) bravely
(c) boldly (d) quickly

5. I brush my teeth ....

(a) sometimes (b) daily
(c) often (d) never

Directions (Q. Nos. 6-10) Given below are some questions and their answers have a blank to be filled with an adverb. Choose the suitable word.

6. How often do you see movies?
I see movies only ....

(a) always (b) never
(c) daily (d) sometimes

7. How often do your parents go on a holiday?
My parents go on a holiday ....

(a) never (b) frequently
(c) always (d) daily

8. How does the tiger run?
The tiger runs ....
(a) slowly (b) sharply
(c) quickly (d) smilingly

9. How did you recite the poem?
I recited the poem ....
(a) closely
(b) foolishly
(c) mildly
(d) loudly

10. How did the old man walk?
The old man walked ....
(a) quickly (b) fastly
(c) slowly (d) sadly

Directions (Q. Nos. 11-15) Choose the correct adverb in the following sentences.

11. You must answer the policeman politely.
(a) must (b) politely
(c) answer (d) policeman

12. Please drink your soup carefully.
(a) Please (b) eat
(c) carefully (d) soup

13. Suddenly he got up and rushed to school.
(a) rushed (b) school
(c) Suddenly (d) got up

14. I want you to reach home safely.
(a) I (b) want
(c) reach (d) safely

15. Roshan always obeyed his teachers and parents.
(a) obeyed
(b) always
(c) teachers
(d) and

Directions (Q. Nos. 16-20) Read the sentences given below and choose the opposite adverb of the underlined adverb.

16. It rained very <u>lightly</u>.
(a) harshly (b) heavily
(c) madly (d) loudly

17. The monkeys chatted <u>noisily</u>.
(a) calmly (b) quietly
(c) softly (d) loudly

18. The policeman talked to my father very <u>rudely</u>.
(a) softly (b) angrily
(c) politely (d) gently

19. The plane landed <u>speedily</u>.
(a) slowly (b) softly
(c) harshly (d) suddenly

20. We all looked at the man <u>usually</u>.
(a) blindly
(b) surprisingly
(c) closily
(d) solidly

21. Match the following adverbs with their type.

List I	List II
A. Carefully	1. Adverbs of Place
B. Often	2. Adverbs of Time
C. Tomorrow	3. Adverbs of Manner
D. Under	4. Adverbs of Frequency

Codes

	A	B	C	D
(a)	3	2	1	4
(b)	3	4	2	1
(c)	3	2	4	1
(d)	2	3	4	1

Directions (Q. Nos. 22-25) Read the passage given below and fill in the blanks with suitable adverbs from the options.

It was Christmas eve. Children were ...**(22)**... waiting for Santa's arrival. They were ...**(23)**... dressed in new clothes. At last, they heard a sound. The shining reindeer ran ...**(24)**... into position at the head of Santa's sleigh. Children cheered ...**(25)**... as Santa started distributing gifts among the children. After receiving gifts from Santa, all children went to their homes and slept peacefully.

22. (a) at once
(b) eagerly
(c) anxiously
(d) happily

23. (a) beautifully (b) brightly
(c) nicely (d) poorly

24. (a) immediately (b) quickly
(c) at once (d) loudly

25. (a) loudly
(b) happy
(c) unhappily
(d) playfully

26. Read the passage and count the number of adverbs.

The birds were chirping noisily. The hunter went up the tree quietly. He wanted to catch atleast 2 birds today. He was very good at catching birds.

(a) 3
(b) 2
(c) 1
(d) None of the above

Chapter 05

Adjectives

Directions (Q. Nos. 1-5) Fill in the blanks with suitable adjective.

1. An elephant is a .... animal.

(a) small (b) big
(c) tall (d) long

2. A rat is a .... animal.

(a) small (b) short
(c) big (d) huge

3. The monkey has a .... tail.

(a) small (b) tall
(c) big (d) long

4. A candy tastes ....

(a) spicy (b) sour
(c) sweet (d) salty

5. The pencil is ....

(a) sharp (b) big
(c) long (d) small

Directions (Q. Nos. 6-10) Find out the adjective in the given sentences.

6. Rajeev is an honest boy.
(a) Rajeev (b) honest
(c) boy (d) None of these

7. Sunaina wears a yellow dress.
(a) Sunaina (b) wears
(c) yellow (d) dress

8. The girl is playing with a beautiful doll.
(a) girl
(b) with
(c) doll
(d) beautiful

9. There are four members in the family.

(a) There (b) four
(c) members (d) family

10. The teacher is very angry today.

(a) The (b) teacher
(c) very (d) angry

Directions (Q. Nos. 11-15) Choose the adjective in the options given below.

11. (a) Cleverness (b) Clever
(c) Cleverly (d) All of these

12. (a) Beautiful (b) Beauty
(c) Beautician (d) Beautifully

13. (a) Health (b) Healthy
(c) Both (a) and (b) (d) None of these

14. (a) Sweety (b) Sweetness
(c) Sweet (d) All of these

15. (a) One (b) First
(c) Both (a) and (b) (d) None of these

Directions (Q. Nos. 16-20) Fill in the blanks with correct degree of adjectives.

16. The giraffe has a .... neck.

(a) longest (b) long
(c) longer (d) most long

17. The baby elephant is growing fatter and .... every day.

(a) heavy (b) heaviest
(c) heavier (d) more heavy

18. The diamond is the .... metal.

(a) costliest (b) costly
(c) costlier (d) more costly

19. I am feeling very .... as I have not eaten any thing.

(a) hungriest (b) hungry
(c) hungrier (d) most hungry

20. This necklace is ....

(a) most beautiful (b) more beautiful
(c) beautiful (d) beautifullest

21. Match the following.

List I	List II
A. Knife	1. Sticky
B. Glue	2. Fast
C. Thunder	3. Sharp
D. Train	4. Loud

Codes

	A	B	C	D
(a)	1	2	3	4
(b)	4	2	1	3
(c)	3	4	2	1
(d)	3	1	4	2

Directions (Q. Nos. 22-25) Read each sentence and choose the opposite adjective of underlined adjective given in the sentences.

22. My father is very <u>tall</u> but my mother is ....

(a) fat (b) big
(c) small (d) short

23. Naina loves <u>cold</u> coffee and .... pizza.

(a) warm (b) roasted
(c) hot (d) tasty

24. The paper is not <u>easy,</u> it is quite ....

(a) difficult
(b) hard
(c) confusing
(d) boring

25. Read the passage and count the number of adjectives.

Ram is a brave and handsome man. He loves Gargi. Gargi is a pretty, young girl. She also likes Ram. They both make a good looking pair.

(a) 4 (b) 5
(c) 6 (d) 3

Directions (Q. Nos. 26-30) Choose the possessive adjectives to fill in the blanks.

26. .... shirt is green.

(a) My
(b) Mine
(c) Yours
(d) Theirs

27. We began .... work at noon.

(a) his
(b) her
(c) our
(d) their

28. .... house is near the city.

(a) Ours (b) Mine
(c) Theirs (d) Their

29. .... teeth are very sharp.

(a) Hers (b) Its
(c) Ours (d) Their

30. The dog is ....

(a) my (b) its
(c) hers (d) our

Chapter 06

Articles

Directions (Q. Nos. 1-10) Fill in the blanks with appropriate articles (**a**, **an**, **the** or **no article**).

1. He is .... police officer.

(a) a (b) an
(c) the (d) No article

2. Mr Sohan is .... teacher.

(a) a (b) an
(c) the (d) No article

3. John is .... electrician.

(a) a (b) an
(c) the (d) No article

4. .... owl is .... bird.

(a) An, an (b) A, the
(c) An, a (d) The, an

5. ..... cat is on ...... roof.

(a) An, a (b) The, a
(c) A, the (d) The, the

6. I have built .... ship.

(a) an (b) the
(c) a (d) None of these

7. .... elephant eats lots of vegetables.

(a) A (b) An
(c) The (d) None of these

8. ...... snake is in ..... room.

(a) A, a (b) A, the
(c) The, a (d) None of these

9. .... dog is sleeping in my room.

(a) An (b) A
(c) The (d) None of these

10. ...... apple ...... day is good for all.

(a) An, the
(b) A, an
(c) An, a
(d) None of the above

Directions (Q. Nos. 11-14) Choose the article for the pictures given below.

11.

(a) A (b) An
(c) The (d) None of these

12.

(a) A (b) An
(c) The (d) None of these

13.

(a) A (b) An
(c) The (d) None of these

14.

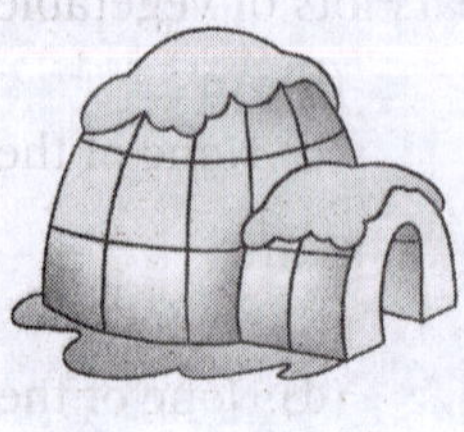

(a) A
(b) The
(c) An
(d) None of these

Directions (Q. Nos. 15-18) Choose the correct sentence from the sentences given below.

15.

(a) I ate a pear in the morning.
(b) I ate the pear in a morning.
(c) I ate an pear in the morning.
(d) I ate a pear in an morning.

16.

(a) Eggs are in an basket.
(b) An eggs are in the basket.
(c) Eggs are in the basket.
(d) An eggs are in a basket.

17.

(a) We live in a expensive home.
(b) We live in an expensive home.
(c) We live in the expensive home.
(d) All of the above are correct

18.

(a) I caught a fish from the lake.
(b) I caught the fish from a lake.
(c) I caught the fish from an lake.
(d) I caught fish from lake.

19. Match the following.

List I	List II
A. Aeroplane	1. A
B. One-rupee coin	2. No article
C. Qutub Minar	3. An
D. Ice cream	4. The

Codes

	A	B	C	D
(a)	1	2	3	4
(b)	3	1	4	2
(c)	2	4	1	3
(d)	4	3	2	1

Directions (Q. Nos. 20-23) Look at the pictures and fill in the blanks with the correct use of article.

20. What is on the table?

There is .... inkpot on the table.

(a) a
(b) an
(c) the
(d) No article

21. Why is Agra famous?

Agra is famous for .... Taj Mahal.

(a) a (b) an
(c) the (d) No article

22. Where does Sophia work?

Sophia works in .... restaurant.

(a) a (b) an
(c) the (d) No article

23. What is the boy eating?

The boy is eating .... apple.

(a) a (b) an
(c) the (d) No article

Directions (Q. Nos. 24-28) Choose the correct article for the pictures given below.

24.

.... Eiffel Tower.

(a) A (b) An
(c) The (d) No article

25.

.... house.

(a) A (b) An
(c) The (d) No article

26.

.... ant-eater.

(a) A (b) An
(c) The (d) No article

27.

.... parrot.

(a) A (b) An
(c) the (d) No article

28.

.... milk.

(a) A
(b) An
(c) The
(d) No article

Directions (Q. Nos. 29-36) Read the passage carefully and fill in the blanks with A, An or The.

The Moon goes around ...**(29)**... Earth. The path is called "...**(30)**... orbit." The same side of the Moon always faces the Earth. It takes one month for ...**(31)**... Moon to go around the Earth. The Moon is ...**(32)**... little more than 200000 miles from the Earth. It has ...**(33)**... dry land with no air or water around it. Shining of the Moon in the night is due to the light from ...**(34)**... Sun. ...**(35)**... Sun is many times bigger than the Earth and ...**(36)**... Moon.

29. (a) a (b) the
(c) an (d) No article

30. (a) the (b) a
(c) an (d) No article

31. (a) a (b) an
(c) the (d) No article

32. (a) an (b) a
(c) the (d) No article

33. (a) a (b) an
(c) the (d) No article

34. (a) a (b) the
(c) an (d) No article

35. (a) The (b) A
(c) An (d) No article

36. (a) a (b) the
(c) an (d) No article

Chapter

07

Prepositions

Directions (Q. Nos. 1-5) Look at the pictures and fill the blanks with appropriate preposition from the options given below.

1. Clothes are .... the almirah.

(a) in (b) on (c) under (d) at

2. The dog is .... the table.

(a) under (b) between
(c) behind (d) in

3. The rat is .... the box.

(a) in (b) on (c) under (d) at

4. The man is sitting .... the tree.

(a) in (b) on
(c) behind (d) under

5. The stars shine .... night.

(a) in (b) at
(c) to (d) on

Directions (Q. Nos. 6-10) Fill in the blanks with suitable prepositions.

6. I have a friend who lives .... Spain.

(a) on (b) by
(c) in (d) to

7. The bone is .... the two dogs.

(a) between (b) besides
(c) above (d) on

8. We spent the evening .... home.

(a) to (b) at
(c) for (d) from

9. Michael and Alex were hiding .... the wardrobe.

(a) below (b) under
(c) over (d) inside

10. Is the milk too hot .... you?

(a) from (b) to
(c) by (d) for

Directions (Q. Nos. 11-15) Find the preposition in the sentences given below.

11. A ball is in the tub.

(a) A (b) is
(c) in (d) the

12. The party is at Maria's house.

(a) The (b) is
(c) at (d) None of these

13. The boy is going to school with his sister.

(a) The (b) to
(c) going (d) his

14. The girl is standing near the car.

(a) the (b) is
(c) near (d) All of these

15. Distribute the candies between the children.

(a) the (b) between
(c) Distribute (d) None of these

Directions (Q. Nos. 16-20) Look at the pictures and find the correct sentence out of the following.

16.

(a) The cake is in the oven.
(b) The cake is behind the oven.
(c) The cake is near the oven.
(d) The cake is between the oven.

17.

(a) The pen is in the pillow.
(b) The pen is to the pillow.
(c) The pen is on the pillow.
(d) The pen is infront of the pillow.

18.

(a) The girl is standing in the boys.
(b) The girl is standing between the boys.
(c) The girl is standing near the boys.
(d) The girl is standing behind the boys.

19.

(a) The Sun is on the cloud.
(b) The Sun is between the cloud.
(c) The Sun is in the cloud.
(d) The Sun is above the cloud.

20.

(a) The cat is next to the wool
(b) The cat is behind the wool.
(c) The cat is under the wool.
(d) The cat is on the wool.

21. Match the following.

	List I		List II
A.	We go .... school for study.	1.	at
B.	The train arrives .... the platform.	2.	between
C.	The Sun rises .... the sky.	3.	to
D.	There is a river......... the two cities.	4.	in

Codes

	A	B	C	D
(a)	3	1	4	2
(b)	2	3	1	4
(c)	4	2	1	3
(d)	1	2	3	4

22. Match the pictures with the preposition related to the 'Rat'.

	List I		List II
A.		1.	Above
B.		2.	Infront of
C.		3.	Behind
D.		4.	Between

Codes

	A	B	C	D
(a)	1	2	3	4
(b)	2	3	4	1
(c)	4	3	2	1
(d)	3	2	1	4

Directions (Q. Nos. 23-26) Find the odd one out.

23. (a) Behind (b) Before (c) Between (d) Because

24. (a) At (b) In (c) On (d) Or

25. (a) Near (b) Farm (c) From (d) For

26. (a) Over (b) Above (c) About (d) Never

Directions (Q. Nos. 27-29) Look at the picture and answer the questions carefully.

27. The clock is .... the wall.
(a) in (b) behind
(c) on (d) over

28. The chair is .... the table.
(a) next to (b) under
(c) above (d) behind

29. The ball is .... the table.
(a) on (b) in
(c) under (d) next to

30. Read the passage and count the number of prepositions.

Navya is hiding under the table. She is playing hide-and-seek with her friend Tara. A vase is kept on the table. Tara came near the table but she could not spot Navya.

(a) 2 (b) 3 (c) 5 (d) 4

Chapter 08

Conjunctions

Directions (Q. Nos. 1-5) Choose the conjunction from the options given below.

1. (a) From (b) Far (c) Farm (d) For
2. (a) Or (b) On (c) An (d) At
3. (a) Not (b) Nor (c) No (d) None of these
4. (a) A (b) An (c) On (d) None of these
5. (a) Yet (b) But (c) Both (a) and (b) (d) None of these

Directions (Q. Nos. 6-10) Choose the conjunction in the given sentences.

6. The music was loud and fast.
(a) the (b) was (c) and (d) None of these
7. You can drink coffee or cold drink now.
(a) you (b) or (c) cold (d) now
8. Fans love to listen Shreya, for she sings beautifully.
(a) love (b) listen (c) for (d) sings
9. Neither Rohan nor Sohan has broken the window.
(a) Rohan (b) neither (c) has (d) broken
10. I wanted to ride my bike but the tire was flat.
(a) to (b) ride (c) but (d) flat

Directions (Q. Nos. 11-15) Fill in the blanks with an appropriate conjunction.

11. Sonia .... her friends go to school by bus.
(a) and (b) so (c) yet (d) or
12. The book contains 200 pages .... I read only 20 pages.
(a) and (b) nor (c) for (d) but
13. Maria is not allowed to watch TV .... play outside by her parents.
(a) and (b) or (c) so (d) but
14. Sonam forgot her notebook at school, ... she couldn't do her homework.
(a) and (b) or (c) so (d) but
15. He is ill .... he is eating fast food.
(a) but
(b) yet
(c) or
(d) and

Directions (Q. Nos. 16-20) Choose the most correct sentence from the options given below.

16. (a) I like to eat apples but not bananas.
(b) I like to eat apples and not bananas.
(c) I like to eat apples so not bananas.
(d) I like to eat apples yet not bananas.

17. (a) My father bought me a jeans or a t-shirt.
(b) My father bought me a jeans and a t-shirt.
(c) My father bought me a jeans so a t-shirt.
(d) My father bought me a jeans but a t-shirt.

18. (a) We played well but we won the match.
(b) We played well yet we won the match.
(c) We played well and we won the match.
(d) We played well so we won the match.

19. (a) Is that rose and lotus?
(b) Is that rose but lotus?
(c) Is that rose or lotus?
(d) Is that rose for lotus?

20. (a) The zebra has black and white stripes.
(b) The zebra has black or white stripes.
(c) The zebra has black but white stripes.
(d) The zebra has black yet white stripes.

Directions (Q. Nos. 21-25) Choose the pair that goes together.

21. (a) He went to the hospital because he hurt his leg.
(b) He went to the hospital and he hurt his leg.
(c) He went to the hospital but he hurt his leg.
(d) He went to the hospital so he hurt his leg.

22. (a) I will study everyday, because I can pass the test.
(b) I will study everyday from I can pass the test.
(c) I will study everyday after I can pass the test.
(d) I will study everyday, so I can pass the test.

23. (a) He is rich and he is not happy.
(b) He is rich yet he is not happy.
(c) He is rich before he is not happy.
(d) He is rich then he is not happy.

24. (a) I could go on the ride so I was taller.
(b) I could go on the ride and I was taller.
(c) I could go on the ride if I was taller.
(d) I could go on the ride or I was taller.

25. (a) We slept because our mom wake us up.
(b) We slept then air mom woke us up.
(c) We slept or our mom woke us up.
(d) We slept until our mom woke us up.

Directions (Q. Nos. 26-31) Choose the correct conjunctions from the following options to complete the sentences.

26. I want to eat a mango .... a banana, ... there is no fruit in the fridge.
(a) and, yet (b) or, but
(c) and, or (d) but, yet

27. I need a pen .... a pencil .... a piece of paper to write a letter to my father.
(a) and, and (b) for, and
(c) or, and (d) yet, but

28. You were driving fast, ... you .... your friend got injured.
(a) for, yet
(b) so, but
(c) or, and
(d) so, and

29. Meenu ate 10 pastries .... 5 pies .... she is hungry.

(a) and, yet
(b) or, but
(c) so, for
(d) and, or

30. Rahul is not a lazy man .... he doesn't think to earn his bread .... butter.

(a) yet, or (b) but, and
(c) for, so (d) nor, and

31. She is very rich .... beautiful .... she is not happy.

(a) and, but
(b) but, and
(c) yet, and
(d) yet, for

Directions (Q. Nos. 32-35) Read the passage and fill in the blanks with suitable conjunctions.

A rich man once found out that his precious ring was stolen ...**(32)**... he called all his servants. He asked them about the ring ...**(33)**... everyone said that they knew nothing about it. The rich man called Birbal ...**(34)**... asked him to find out the thief. Birbal played a trick. The next morning, the thief was caught ...**(35)**... he was not able to understand Birbal's plan.

32. (a) yet (b) but
(c) so (d) and

33. (a) yet (b) but
(c) and (d) for

34. (a) so (b) and
(c) or (d) yet

35. (a) yet (b) as
(c) so (d) for

36. Read the passage and count the number of conjunctions.

Ram and Shyam are good friends. Ram likes to play but Shyam likes to study. Neither Ram nor Shyam like to watch movies.

(a) 3
(b) 4
(c) 5
(d) 6

Chapter 09

Punctuations

Directions (Q. Nos. 1-5) Look at the picture and select the correctly written word.

1. 

(a) butterflies (b) Butterflies
(c) butterflie (d) butterFlies

2. 

(a) india Gate
(b) iNdia gAte
(c) India Gate
(d) India gate

3. 

(a) ABDUL Kalam (b) Abdul KALAM
(c) abdul kalam (d) Abdul Kalam

4. 

(a) INDIA'S MAP (b) India's Map
(c) India's map (d) india's Map

5. 

(a) a Police man
(b) A Policeman
(c) A POLICE MAN
(d) a Police Man

Directions (Q. Nos. 6-10) Choose the correct word to fill in the blank in the given sentences.

6. .... are like a father figure for me.

(a) you
(b) You
(c) YoU
(d) None of the above

7. .... is the capital of India.
(a) delhi (b) DELHI
(c) Delhi (d) All of these

8. The .... is our holy river.
(a) ganges (b) Ganges
(c) GANGES (d) Ganges

9. .... was built by Shah Jahan.
(a) Taj Mahal
(b) taj Mahal
(c) Taj mahal
(d) tajmahal

10. .... is my best friend.
(a) john (b) JoHN
(c) John (d) johN

Directions (Q. Nos. 11-15) Fill in the blank with suitable punctuation marks in each sentence given below. Choose from the options.

11. My favourite colour is yellow ....
(a) (.) (b) (?)
(c) (,) (d) None of these

12. How high can you jump ....
(a) (,) (b) (.)
(c) (?) (d) capital letter

13. Our school is situated far from city ....
(a) (?)
(b) (.)
(c) (,)
(d) capital letter

14. Gunjan brushed her teeth .... washed her face and got ready ....
(a) (? ,) (b) (, ?)
(c) (, .) (d) (? ?)

15. No .... he has not finished his home work.
(a) (.) (b) (,)
(c) (?) (d) capital letter

Directions (Q. Nos. 16-20) Choose the correct sentence from the options given below.

16. (a) jim is a little kid?
(b) JIM is a little kid.
(c) Jim is a little kid.
(d) Jim is a little Kid,

17. (a) You and i will study together.
(b) you and i will study together.
(c) you and I will study together.
(d) You and I will study together.

18. (a) English is a global language?
(b) English is a global language.
(c) English is a global language,
(d) english is a global language.

19. (a) Rashmi teaches in a school?
(b) Rashmi teaches in a school.
(c) rashmi teaches in a school.
(d) RASHMI teaches in a school?

20. (a) My Father works in a government office.
(b) My FATHER works in a Government Office,
(c) My father works in a government office?
(d) My father works in a government office.

21. Match the following.

	List I		List II
A.	Inverted comma	1.	(?)
B.	Comma	2.	(“ ”)
C.	Exclamatory Mark	3.	(,)
D.	Question Mark	4.	(!)

Codes

	A	B	C	D		A	B	C	D
(a)	4	2	3	1	(b)	3	1	2	4
(c)	2	3	4	1	(d)	2	4	1	3

Directions (Q. Nos. 22-26) Read the passage carefully and fill the blanks with correct punctuation marks.

One day Danny went with his father to a zoo ...**(22)**... . He was very excited to see different types of birds and animals. After a while ...**(23)**... they came in front of the cage of a lion.

The lion was moving here and there in his cage. Danny asked his father, what will happen if the lion came out of the cage and ate him up ...**(24)**... He did not know how to get back home. At least he should tell him the route to reach home.

Danny....**(25)**...s father laughed at the innocent question of his son ...**(26)**...

22. (a) (,) (b) (?) (c) (.) (d) None of these

23. (a) (?) (b) (.) (c) (,) (d) None of these

24. (a) (.) (b) (?) (c) (,) (d) None of these

25. (a) (?) (b) (,) (c) (’) (d) None of these

26. (a) (,) (b) (!) (c) (.) (d) (?)

Chapter 10

Sentences

Directions (Q. Nos. 1-5) Identify the subject of the given sentences.

1. Mango is called the king of fruits.
   (a) Mango (b) king
   (c) fruits (d) called

2. Elephants live in the jungle.
   (a) jungle (b) live
   (c) Elephants (d) None of these

3. Rahul and Preeti are going for a picnic.
   (a) going
   (b) picnic
   (c) Rahul and Preeti
   (d) Preeti

4. My bottle is green in colour.
   (a) My (b) My bottle
   (c) green (d) colour

5. You are not going for a movie.
   (a) going (b) movie
   (c) not (d) You

Directions (Q. Nos. 6-11) Identify the predicate of the given sentences.

6. Sarah goes to school.
   (a) Sarah (b) goes
   (c) goes to school (d) to school

7. I have finished my lunch.
   (a) finished
   (b) have finished my lunch
   (c) I
   (d) my lunch

8. My brother lives in India.
   (a) lives in India
   (b) My brother
   (c) lives in
   (d) My brother lives in

9. My computer is not working.
   (a) not working
   (b) My computer
   (c) computer is not working
   (d) is not working

10. A dog is wagging its tail.
   (a) A dog
   (b) is wagging its tail
   (c) wagging its tails
   (d) its tail

11. Prisha is singing a song.
   (a) Prisha is
   (b) is singing a song
   (c) singing
   (d) a song

Directions (Q. Nos. 12-16) Look at the images and choose the correct negative sentence.

12.

(a) The boy is flying a kite.
(b) The boy is not flying a kite.
(c) The boy is flying not a kite.
(d) Is the boy flying a kite?

13.

(a) The man is very fat.
(b) The man is very thin.
(c) The man is not thin.
(d) Is the man very fat?

14.

(a) The cat is catching a mouse.
(b) The cat is relaxing.
(c) The cat is not catching a mouse.
(d) The cat is on the floor.

15.

(a) The boy looks very happy.
(b) The boy is very angry.
(c) The boy is neither happy nor angry.
(d) The boy is sad.

16.

(a) The child is hungry.
(b) The child is playing.
(c) The child is not hungry.
(d) Is the child hungry?

Directions (Q. Nos. 17-20) See the pictures and choose the correct interrogative sentence.

17.

(a) What is the boy thinking?
(b) The children are watching something.
(c) The boy is asking a question.
(d) The children are going to school.

18.

(a) I like apples.
(b) Do you like apples?
(c) Eat these apples.
(d) I do not like apples.

19.

(a) Are these your books?
(b) I want to borrow one book.
(c) I like reading books.
(d) Oh! these books are very heavy.

20.

(a) I like this big hat.
(b) I do not like this big hat.
(c) Do you like this big hat?
(d) This hat is very big.

Directions (Q. Nos. 21-25) Choose the correct assertive sentences for the given pictures.

21.

(a) Is a dog sleeping under the table?
(b) A cat is sleeping under the table.
(c) A dog is sleeping under the table.
(d) A dog is not lying under the table.

22.

(a) They are reading books.
(b) They are playing.
(c) Are children playing?
(d) Children are not reading books.

23.

(a) A monkey is not dancing.
(b) A monkey is eating a banana.
(c) A monkey is dancing.
(d) Was a monkey dancing?

24.

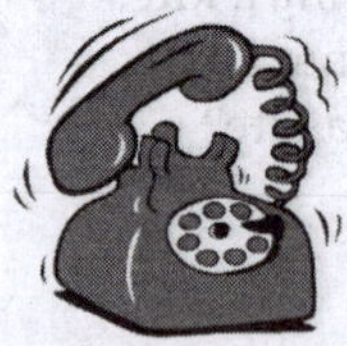

(a) The telephone is ringing.
(b) Is the telephone ringing.
(c) The telephone is not ringing.
(d) Is this a telephone?

25.

(a) A rabbit is lying on the floor.
(b) A rabbit is not jumping.
(c) Is the rabbit sad?
(d) A rabbit is jumping.

Chapter 11

Simple Tenses

Directions (Q. Nos. 1-10) Fill in the blanks with appropriate verbs with their corresponding tense.

1. Anju .... to her college everyday.
(a) goes (b) went
(c) will go (d) go

2. Sapna .... in the school in 2014.
(a) teach (b) teaches
(c) will teach (d) taught

3. Vinu .... a house next month.
(a) buy (b) buys
(c) will buy (d) bought

4. He always .... the car carefully.
(a) drive (b) drives
(c) will drive (d) drove

5. They .... her birthday yesterday.
(a) celebrate (b) celebrates
(c) celebrated (d) will celebrate

6. He .... not take tuition for Maths.
(a) do (b) are
(c) does (d) is

7. They .... not enjoy movies.
(a) is (b) do
(c) does (d) are

8. Robert .... finished his homework.
(a) does (b) has
(c) do (d) have

9. I .... be 10 years old next Sunday.
(a) will (b) is
(c) am (d) has

10. .... they have a big car?
(a) Does (b) Is
(c) Do (d) Are

11. Match the verbs given in list-I with their correct tenses given in list-II.

List I	List II
A. Presents	1. Simple Future Tense
B. Talked	2. Simple Present Tense
C. Will fly	3. Simple Past Tense

Codes

	A	B	C		A	B	C
(a)	1	3	2	(b)	2	1	3
(c)	3	2	1	(d)	2	3	1

12. Match the verbs given in List I with their past forms given in List II.

List I	List II
A. Walk	1. Would
B. Will	2. Tried
C. Tries	3. Walked
D. Reside	4. Resided

Codes

	A	B	C	D		A	B	C	D
(a)	3	1	2	4	(b)	3	1	4	2
(c)	3	4	2	1	(d)	3	4	1	2

Directions (Q. Nos. 13-20) Answer the following questions with the correct use of tense.

13. What do you give him everyday?
I .... him a chocolate everyday.
(a) gives
(b) gave
(c) give
(d) shall give

14. Why did they go to the stadium?
They .... to the stadium to watch the match.
(a) go (b) goes
(c) went (d) will go

15. When will he take his medicine?
He .... his medicine after dinner.
(a) will take (b) take
(c) takes (d) took

16. Does he study daily?
Yes, he .... daily.
(a) study
(b) will study
(c) studies
(d) studied

17. What time is the next flight?
The next flight .... at 8:00 pm.
(a) was (b) are
(c) is (d) were

18. Where will you go during summer holidays?
I .... to Goa during summer holidays.
(a) is go (b) went
(c) will go (d) go

19. How did you spend your Sunday?
I .... my Sunday playing and eating.
(a) spend
(b) spends
(c) spent
(d) was spent

20. What time does he sleep in the night?
He .... at 9:00 pm every night.
(a) is sleeping (b) sleeps
(c) slept (d) will sleep

Directions (Q. Nos. 21-25) Change the verbs in the given sentences into simple past tense.

21. I receive his letter.
(a) Receives (b) Received
(c) Will receive (d) Receive

22. The river flows under the bridge.
(a) Flowed (b) Flown
(c) Flew (d) Flow

23. The aeroplane will land at 3.30 p.m.
(a) Lands (b) Land
(c) Landed (d) Will land

24. Show goes for a walk.
(a) Go (b) Went
(c) Wents (d) Goed

25. He will meet the school principal on Monday.
(a) Meet (b) Meted
(c) Met (d) Meets

Directions (Q. Nos. 26-30) Change the bold verbs in the given sentences into simple future tense.

26. Rohan **eats** his apple for breakfast.
(a) Eat (b) Will eat
(c) Ate (d) Will eats

27. Mehtab **plays** with her toys.
(a) Played (b) Play
(c) Will play (d) Will plays

28. We **study** very carefully during the exams.
(a) Will study (b) Studies
(c) Studied (d) Will studied

29. She **sang** for a musical company.
(a) Sing (b) Sings
(c) Will sing (d) Sung

30. My father **took** me to the park.
(a) Take
(b) Will take
(c) Takes
(d) Will took

Directions (Q. Nos. 31-35) Fill in the cross word.

31. Change the given sentence into simple past tense.
Ram and Shyam **will write** books in English.
(a) written (b) wrote
(c) write (d) No change

32. Change the given sentence into present tense.
He **earned** his livings by selling popcorns.
(a) earn (b) earns
(c) will earn (d) No change

33. Change the given sentence into past tense.
The police **arrest** the thieves.
(a) arrests
(b) arrest
(c) arrested
(d) No change

34. Change the given sentence into present tense.
The Sun **will rise** in the East.
(a) rise (b) rises
(c) rose (d) No change

35. Change the given sentence into past tense.
She **will work** as a nurse.
(a) work (b) works
(c) worked (d) No change

Directions (Q. Nos. 36-40) Read the passage carefully and fill in the blanks with suitable verbs.

Once, a rich boy ...**(36)**... to visit his native village . It was a sunny afternoon and he was feeling very hungry. So, he ...**(37)**... some food from a shop to eat.

Suddenly, he ...**(38)**... a poor boy sitting at a distance and found that he was very hungry. He decided to leave some food for the poor boy.

But, as he was very hungry, he forgot. He ...**(39)**... all the things. When he drank water, he saw something written at the base of the vessel, "Those who don't care for poor have no right to have food."

So, the rich boy bought some food for the poor boy and ...**(40)**... it to him.

36. (a) go (b) went
(c) going (d) goes

37. (a) bought (b) sold
(c) stole (d) snatched

38. (a) see (b) saw
(c) sees (d) will see

39. (a) shall eat (b) eats
(c) eat (d) ate

40. (a) give (b) gives
(c) gave (d) will give

Chapter 12

Words and their Meanings

Directions (Q. Nos. 1-9) Choose the word similar in meaning to the words given below.

1. Glad
(a) Broken (b) Happy
(c) Open (d) Angry

2. Slim
(a) Short (b) Fat
(c) Slender (d) Tall

3. Cold
(a) Hot (b) Cool
(c) Easy (d) Low

4. Fast
(a) Clear (b) Main
(c) Clean (d) Quick

5. Tiny
(a) Loose (b) Big
(c) Small (d) Thick

6. Big
(a) Large (b) Many
(c) Easy (d) Next

7. Wrong
(a) Correct (b) Bad
(c) False (d) Good

8. Over
(a) Behind (b) Under
(c) Above (d) Below

9. Clever
(a) Risky (b) Cunning
(c) Fast (d) Wide

Directions (Q. Nos. 10-14) Choose the word similar in meaning to the underlined words.

10. Maria was feeling very <u>tired</u>.
(a) happy (b) glad
(c) weary (d) small

11. My friend, Paul, belongs to a <u>rich</u> family.
(a) clever (b) tasty
(c) poor (d) wealthy

12. Richa's mother cooks <u>delicious</u> food.
(a) boring (b) unhappy
(c) tasty (d) quick

13. <u>Nice</u> manners always attract people.
(a) Pleasant
(b) Rude
(c) Dishonest
(d) Secure

14. Daniel left his paper <u>blank</u> during Maths exam.

(a) full (b) empty
(c) heavy (d) kind

15. Match the words given in List A with words similar in meaning given in List B.

	List A		List B
A.	Quick	1.	Skinny
B.	Strange	2.	Easy
C.	Simple	3.	Unusual
D.	Thin	4.	Fast

Codes

	A	B	C	D
(a)	2	3	1	4
(b)	3	2	4	1
(c)	4	3	2	1
(d)	2	1	3	4

Directions (Q. Nos. 16-20) Choose the pair of similar words from the given words.

16. Alien, foreigner, break, stop

(a) Alien and break
(b) Foreigner and stop
(c) Break and foreigner
(d) Alien and foreigner

17. Silly, brittle, tough, breakable

(a) Brittle and breakable
(b) Silly and tough
(c) Breakable and silly
(d) Brittle and tough

18. Cheap, dear, weak, inexpensive

(a) Inexpensive and weak
(b) Dear and cheap
(c) Cheap and inexpensive
(d) Dear and weak

19. Rebel, present, gift, old

(a) Rebel and old
(b) Present and gift
(c) Rebel and present
(d) Gift and old

20. True, main, simple, correct

(a) True and main
(b) Main and simple
(c) True and correct
(d) Correct and simple

Directions (Q. Nos. 21-25) Choose the word that means the same as underlined words.

21. The word .... can be similar in meaning to the words '<u>light</u>' and '<u>just</u>'.

(a) blond (b) fair
(c) honest (d) brave

22. The word .... can be similar in meaning to the words '<u>new</u>' and '<u>story</u>'.

(a) film (b) book
(c) novel (d) cinema

23. The word .... can be similar in meaning to the words '<u>flame</u>' and '<u>shoot</u>'.

(a) fire (b) burn
(c) hot (d) high

24. The word __________ can be similar in meaning to the words '<u>okay</u>' and '<u>penalty</u>'.

(a) punishment (b) pleasant
(c) simple (d) fine

25. The word .... can be similar in meaning to the words '<u>complete</u>' and '<u>exhausted</u>'.

(a) finish (b) end
(c) tired (d) begin

Chapter 13

Words and their Opposites

Directions (Q. Nos. 1-9) Choose the correct opposite meaning word from the given words.

1. Pretty

(a) Dry (b) Ugly
(c) Beautiful (d) Crazy

2. Never

(a) Almost (b) Sometimes
(c) Often (d) Always

3. Far

(a) Fly (b) Close
(c) Distance (d) Over

4. Wet

(a) Dry (b) Float
(c) Full (d) Sink

5. Glad

(a) Happy (b) Excited
(c) Sad (d) Shocked

6. End

(a) Finish (b) Bottom
(c) Complete (d) Begin

7. Rude

(a) Polite
(b) Soft spoken
(c) Courteous
(d) Kind

8. Absence

(a) Refuse (b) Presence
(c) Admit (d) Finish

9. Careful

(a) Softly (b) Safe
(c) Careless (d) Dull

Directions (Q. Nos. 10-14) Choose the correct opposite words for the underlined words.

10. He wore very <u>costly</u> clothes.

(a) warm (b) cheap
(c) rich (d) big

11. The small puppy was too <u>weak</u> to walk keep.

(a) great (b) big
(c) strong (d) energy

12. Due to an accident, my servant has an a very <u>ugly</u> face.

(a) crazy (b) cold
(c) beautiful (d) honest

13. My house is very <u>far</u> away.

(a) close
(b) near
(c) full
(d) further

14. My father was very angry to see my report card.
(a) pleasant (b) cold
(c) happy (d) gay

15. Match the words given in List A with their opposites given in List B.

List A	List B
A. Exciting	1. Tasty
B. Playful	2. Depart
C. Arrive	3. Serious
D. Bland	4. Boring

Codes

	A	B	C	D		A	B	C	D
(a)	4	2	1	3	(b)	4	3	2	1
(c)	3	2	1	4	(d)	1	2	3	4

Directions (Q. Nos. 16-20) Choose the pair of opposite words from the given words.

16. Right, dirty, wrong, add
(a) Right and dirty (b) Dirty and add
(c) Right and wrong (d) Wrong and add

17. Clear, heavy, important, light
(a) Clear and important
(b) Light and heavy
(c) Heavy and clear
(d) Important and light

18. Loose, tight, bright, go
(a) Loose and bright
(b) Go and tight
(c) Bright and tight
(d) Loose and tight

19. Old, dry, ugly, young
(a) Old and ugly (b) young and old
(c) Old and young (d) Dry and young

20. Fat, north, left, skinny
(a) Fat and skinny
(b) North and left
(c) Left and skinny
(d) Fat and north

Directions (Q. Nos. 21-25) Fill in the blanks with the opposite word of the underlined words

21. Every time I close the cookie jar, my sneaky brother goes over to .... it.
(a) break (b) tight
(c) open (d) clean

22. When I was little, my sister used to sleep on the .... bunk and I slept on the bottom.
(a) top (b) first
(c) high (d) above

23. When my glass of milk is ...., I fill it up until it is full.
(a) clear (b) hollow
(c) transparent (d) empty

24. The subway travels below the ground and the passenger train ....
(a) low (b) above
(c) high (d) air

25. We go in through the front door and .... through the back door.
(a) exit (b) entry
(c) out (d) All of these

Chapter 14

Jumbled Words

Directions (Q. Nos. 1-25) Given below are words where letters are jumbled. Form a meaningful word from each.

1. SOMUIQOT
(a) Mascot (b) Mosquito
(c) Mosque (d) Muscat

2. GHNINGLEATI
(a) Nightfall (b) Nightly
(c) Nightingale (d) Nighthawk

3. SRLUIRQE
(a) Swirl (b) Square
(c) Quarrel (d) Squirrel

4. LENTAHPE
(a) Elements (b) Elegant
(c) Elephant (d) Evident

5. RECSMA
(a) Screen (b) Scream
(c) Cream (d) Scheme

6. ABLESBLA
(a) Volleyball (b) Valuable
(c) Baseball (d) Squall

7. OIAGLRTLA
(a) Letter (b) Escalator
(c) Alligator (d) Tractor

8. ZMECPAEHIN
(a) Chamelion (b) Camelin
(c) Chimpanzee (d) Champion

9. AMINBDONT
(a) Button (b) Badminton
(c) Cotton (d) Boston

10. AGROPEMTANE
(a) Planet (b) Plantain
(c) Granted (d) Pomegranate

11. TOBOTERE
(a) Reboot (b) Boycott
(c) Beetroot (d) Freeboot

12. FNUSWLROE
(a) Power (b) Shower
(c) Glower (d) Sunflower

13. BALOACBKDR
(a) Aboveboard (b) Blackboard
(c) Keyboard (d) Boulevard

14. CARENETLG
(a) Beagle (b) Angle
(c) Wriggle (d) Rectangle

15. NEISJAM
(a) Mason (b) Jasmine
(c) Ravine (d) Marine

16. FICFUDYLTI
(a) Faculty (b) Daffodil
(c) Difficulty (d) Loyalty

17. UABETIULF
(a) Bountiful (b) Beautiful
(c) Tasteful (d) Blissful

18. CATIRSESA
(a) Staircase (b) Upstairs
(c) Bookcase (d) Showcase

19. LSCUE
(a) Lousy (b) Scale
(c) Clues (d) Class

20. WMISMGNI
(a) Swinging (b) Swaying
(c) Sweating (d) Swimming

21. TYAWEHL
(a) Healthy (b) Worthy
(c) Filthy (d) Wealthy

22. TONMORI
(a) Mortar (b) Monitor
(c) Nectar (d) Traitor

23. FUBETYTLR
(a) Moonlight (b) Freestyle
(c) Butterfly (d) Beautiful

24. NOLEMRETAW
(a) Lemonade (b) Woolen
(c) Waterbottle (d) Watermelon

25. LARRCALTEIP
(a) Calculator (b) Collector
(c) Caterpillar (d) Calendar

Directions (Q. Nos. 26-32) Rearrange the following words to make a correct sentence.

26. Driving/he/very/is/fast
(a) Very fast driving he is.
(b) Is driving he very fast.
(c) He driving very is fast.
(d) He is driving very fast.

27. Story/a/me/please/tell
(a) Please tell me a story.
(b) Tell story a me please.
(c) Please tell a story me.
(d) Story tell me please a.

28. a/seven/there/days/are/in/week
(a) There seven days are in a week.
(b) There seven are days in a week.
(c) There are seven days in a week.
(d) In a week there are seven days.

29. boys/playing/the/the/are/in/garden
(a) The boys in the garden are playing.
(b) Playing are the boys in the garden.
(c) In the garden the boys are playing.
(d) The boys are playing in the garden.

30. shining/are/the/stars/sky/in/the
(a) The stars are shining in the sky.
(b) The stars shining are in the sky.
(c) The stars in the sky are shining.
(d) In the sky the stars are shining.

31. John/Harry/praising/is
(a) Praising John is Harry.
(b) John is praising Harry.
(c) John praising Harry is.
(d) John is Harry praising.

32. Classroom/Jessica's/second/on/is/floor/the
(a) Is on the second floor Jessica's classroom.
(b) Jessica's floor is on the second classroom.
(c) Jessica's classroom is on the second floor.
(d) Jessica's second floor is on the classroom.

Chapter 15

Word Pairs and Odd One Out

Directions (Q. Nos. 1-10) Choose the correct word pairs.

1. (a) Bits and pieces (b) Bread but butter
(c) Up with down (d) Right when left

2. (a) Facts but figures (b) Give and take
(c) Day while night (d) Heaven by hell

3. (a) Husband of wife
(b) Bride and bridegroom
(c) Law or order
(d) In on out

4. (a) Life in death (b) Part to parcel
(c) Push and pull (d) Rise for fall

5. (a) Salt on pepper (b) Ups for downs
(c) Come when go (d) Wear and tear

6. (a) Bread and butter (b) Cut or run
(c) Read by write (d) Stop not start

7. (a) Again in again (b) By and large
(c) Bed or breakfast (d) Profit by loss

8. (a) Pen not pencil
(b) Bacon but eggs
(c) Name but address
(d) Rise and shine

9. (a) First or last (b) Shoes in socks
(c) Sooner or later (d) Soap on water

10. (a) Knife or fork (b) Wait and watch
(c) War but peace (d) Off or on

Directions (Q. Nos. 11-15) Choose the incorrect word pair.

11. (a) Black and white
(b) Forgive and forget
(c) Length and breadth
(d) High with low

12. (a) Here and there (b) Now and then
(c) Black by white (d) Back and forth

13. (a) Hot and cold (b) Safe for secure
(c) Lock and key (d) Cats and dogs

14. (a) To or fro
(b) Thick and thin
(c) Over and out
(d) Now and again

15. (a) Far and wide
(b) Down of out
(c) First and foremost
(d) Hard and fast

Directions (Q. Nos. 16-20) Complete the word pairs.

16. Mother and ....

(a) Husband (b) Sister
(c) Daughter (d) Father

17. Cup and ....

(a) Spoon (b) Saucer
(c) Glass (d) Bowl

18. .... and above.

(a) Below (b) Ground
(c) There (d) Over

19. .... and sugar.

(a) Spice (b) Cream
(c) Spoon (d) Cereal

20. Hammer and ....

(a) Nail (b) Nale
(c) Axe (d) Saw

Directions (Q. Nos. 21-28) Choose the odd word out of the given options in each.

21. Beautiful, Monkey, Pretty, Ugly, Simple

(a) Beautiful
(b) Ugly
(c) Pretty
(d) Monkey

22. Table, Bed, Chair, Wood, Door

(a) Table (b) Chair
(c) Wood (d) Bed

23. Walk, Sit, Run, Jogging, Eat

(a) Walk (b) Run
(c) Sit (d) Jogging

24. Sparrow, Eagle, Aeroplane, Squirrel, Cloud

(a) Eagle
(b) Squirrel
(c) Aeroplane
(d) Cloud

25. Deer, Cow, Lion, Sheep, Goat

(a) Cow (b) Goat
(c) Sheep (d) Lion

26. Round, Oval, Square, Triangle, Golden

(a) Round (b) Golden
(c) Square (d) Triangle

27. Orange, Apple, Grapes, Ball, Banana

(a) Orange
(b) Ball
(c) Banana
(d) Apple

28. Den, Nest, Roof, Cave, Burrow

(a) Den (b) Roof
(c) Burrow (d) Nest

Directions (Q. Nos. 29-34) Find the odd one out.

29.

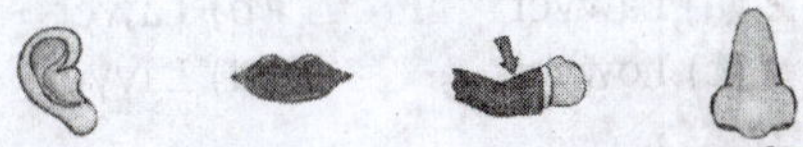

(a) (b) (c) (d)

30.

(a) (b) (c) (d)

31.

(a) (b) (c) (d)

32.

(a) (b) (c) (d)

33.

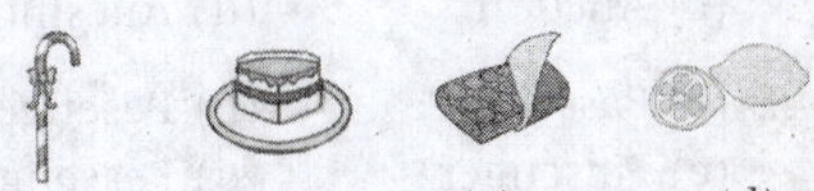

(a) (b) (c) (d)

34.

sleep (a) sheep (b) jeep (c) car (d)

Chapter 16

Spelling Test

Directions (Q. Nos. 1-10) Choose the correct spelling.

1. (a) Famus (b) Famos (c) Femus (d) Famous
2. (a) Lawyer (b) Lawer (c) Lowyer (d) Layyer
3. (a) Pumkin (b) Pumpkin (c) Pampkin (d) Pamkin
4. (a) Pandamic (b) Pandamec (c) Pandemic (d) Pendamic
5. (a) Explorar (b) Explorer (c) Explaurer (d) Xplorer
6. (a) Building (b) Bilding (c) Buildeing (d) Belding
7. (a) Carefull (b) Careful (c) Cerefull (d) Cereful
8. (a) Oction (b) Ouction (c) Auction (d) Aucshion
9. (a) Passenger (b) Pesenger (c) Paisenger (d) Pessengar
10. (a) Firfightar (b) Firefighter (c) Fairfighter (d) Firefaiter

Directions (Q. Nos. 11-20) Choose the wrongly spelt word.

11. (a) Preparation (b) Curant (c) Policeman (d) Smiling
12. (a) Painting (b) Farmer (c) Gramar (d) Hammer
13. (a) Octopus (b) Classes (c) Helmet (d) Scuter
14. (a) Simple (b) Beautiful (c) Claver (d) Ladder
15. (a) Staircese (b) Balcony (c) Victory (d) Humanity
16. (a) Homely (b) Panguin (c) Theatre (d) Video
17. (a) Remamber (b) Encourage (c) Because (d) Teaser
18. (a) Newspaper (b) Calinder (c) Cylinder (d) Campfire
19. (a) Triangle (b) Picture (c) Trully (d) Happily
20. (a) Responsible (b) Desktop (c) Mobile (d) Camputar

Directions (Q. Nos. 21-30) Fill in the blanks with correctly spelt words.

21. Put a .... of water on the stove.

(a) kattle (b) kettle
(c) ketle (d) cattle

22. The girl threaded the .... for her mother.

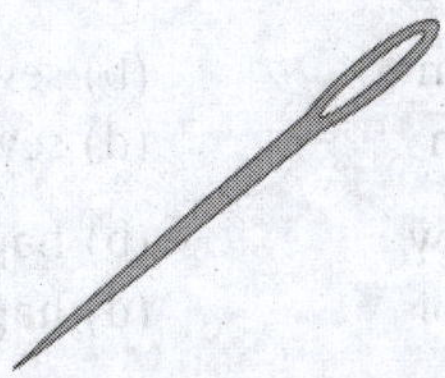

(a) needle (b) nidle
(c) needal (d) needel

23. The .... is characterised by its very long neck.

(a) girraf (b) girraffe
(c) giraffe (d) jiraffe

24. The clown was wearing a blue .... and an orange shirt.

(a) trauser (b) trauzer
(c) trouzer (d) trouser

25. I love my ....

(a) grandfader
(b) grandfather
(c) grendfather
(d) graindfather

26. The .... has laid in a store of nuts for the winter.

(a) squiral
(b) squirral
(c) squarrel
(d) squirrel

27. We celebrated Rani's 6th ....

(a) barthday
(b) budday
(c) birthday
(d) birdday

28. I love eating ....

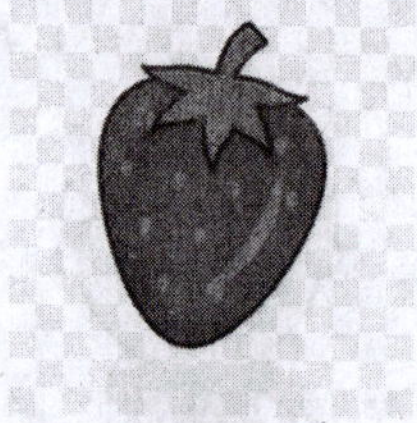

(a) strawberry
(b) strowbery
(c) strawbery
(d) strewbarry

29. A big .... had come out of the river.

(a) crocodail
(b) crkodile
(c) crocodile
(d) krocodail

30. We saw two .... near the shore.

(a) dollphins
(b) daulphins
(c) dolfins
(d) dolphins

Directions (Q. Nos. 31-40) fill in the blanks with correct spellings.

.....**(31)**..... is my birthday. I am .....**(32)**..... years old. I am very .....**(33)**..... . My parents gave me a .....**(34)**..... . My .....**(35)**..... gave me a kite. My sister gave me a .....**(36)**..... rope. My grandmother gave me a .....**(37)**..... . My best .....**(38)**..... gave me a teddy bear. I have a cake with .....**(39)**..... . I ate it with my hands. I ..... **(40)**..... a lot.

31. (a) Tuday (b) Todey (c) Today (d) Tooday

32. (a) saven (b) sevin (c) siven (d) seven

33. (a) heppy (b) happy (c) happi (d) hapy

34. (a) bicycle (b) baicicle (c) bycicle (d) bycycall

35. (a) brathar (b) brother (c) brather (d) birather

36. (a) skepping (b) skiping (c) skipping (d) skeping

37. (a) puzal (b) puzzel (c) pussel (d) puzzle

38. (a) frend (b) frand (c) friend (d) freind

39. (a) candals (b) candles (c) candils (d) cendels

40. (a) enjoyed (b) enjoyid (c) injoyed (d) injjoy

Chapter 17

Reading Comprehension

Directions (Q. Nos. 1-26) Read the passages given below and answer the questions that follows.

Passage 1

The hummingbird is a tiny bird. It is so light it can sit on a flower. No other bird is so small.

A hummingbird's nest would fit into one side of a nut shell. It holds two eggs. The eggs are as tiny as bees. Four baby hummingbirds would fit in a teaspoon.

It flies like a helicopter and its wings make a humming sound. That's how it got its name.

1. How many baby hummingbirds would fit in a tea spoon?
(a) 2 (b) 3 (c) 4 (d) 5

2. Hummingbird's eggs are as tiny as ....
(a) bees (b) buds
(c) nut (d) None of these

3. Choose the antonym of 'light' in the context of the passage.
(a) dark (b) heavy (c) bright (d) tiny

4. Choose the synonym of the word 'tiny' in the context of the passage.
(a) large (b) huge (c) thick (d) small

5. The bird smaller than a hummingbird is ....
(a) wren
(b) robin
(c) bluebird
(d) None of the above

Passage 2

First Airplane Trip

Jake is going on a trip. He and Mom take a taxi to the airport.

"It's my first plane trip," he tells the taxi driver.

"That's great!" the taxi driver says.

Jake rolls his suitcase onto the plane.

"It's my first plane trip," he tells the pilot.

"Welcome aboard," the pilot says.

Jake finds his seat and buckles his seatbelt.

The plane's engines rumble and roar. Jake opens his backpack and pulls out Panda.

"It's my first plane trip," he whispers. He holds Panda's paw.

The plane moves faster and faster.

Then—Whoosh! On the ground, cars and houses look like toys.

Jake smiles. "Guess what, Panda?" he says, "Flying is fun!"

6. Jake and his mom hire .... to travel to the airport.
(a) a plane (b) a taxi
(c) a car (d) a bus

7. Jake was excited as it was his ....
(a) first taxi trip (b) first ship trip
(c) first train trip (d) first plane trip

8. In the story, Panda is ....
(a) Jake's brother (b) Jake's friend
(c) a stuffed toy (d) an animal

9. Choose the antonym of 'buckle' in the context of the passage.
(a) fastening (b) tight
(c) catch (d) loose

10. Choose the word/group of words which gives similar meaning as 'look like toys' according to the passage.
(a) very small (b) very far
(c) very beautiful (d) very bad

Passage 3

The Three Fishes

These fish have names.
This is Finny.
Finny has beautiful long fins that help her swim fast.
This is Tayla.
Tayla's big tail moves from side to side and it helps her to go this way or that way.
This is Igor.
Igor has great big eyes.
Igor's great big eyes help him to see where he is going and they also help him to see big scary fish!

11. .... has beautiful long fins.
(a) Finny
(b) Tayla
(c) Igor
(d) None of the above

12. Igor has ....
(a) big fins (b) big tail
(c) big eyes (d) None of these

13. Find the antonym of 'long' from the options given below.
(a) short (b) big
(c) small (d) huge

14. Choose the synonym of 'scary' from the options given below.
(a) large (b) powerful
(c) horrifying (d) normal

Passage 4

The Sun and the Moon

One day the Sun said to the Moon,
"I shine in the day so the people on Earth can see."
"I give energy to all the plants and animals. It takes Earth a whole year to go around me."
The Moon said, "I am sometimes in the sky in the day time and sometimes at night."
"I have lots of mountains and I also have big craters. I make the tides in the sea. It takes me one month to go around Earth."

15. The .... gives energy to animals and ....
(a) Moon, plants (b) Sun, people
(c) Sun, Moon (d) Sun, plants

16. The .... takes .... to go around Earth.
(a) Sun, one year
(b) Moon, one month
(c) Sun, one month
(d) Moon, one year

17. Choose the antonym of 'day' from the given options.
(a) night (b) dark
(c) gloomy (d) light

18. Choose the synonym of 'big' from the options given below.

(a) long (b) small
(c) huge (d) tiny

Passage 5

The Apple and the Banana

One day an apple said to a banana,

"You are shaped like the Moon."

The banana said, "Yes, I know, and I'm also the same colour as the Moon."

The apple said, "I'm bright red. Some of my family are green and some are yellow like you.

When people eat me it makes a crunchy sound. That's because I'm hard."

The banana said, "When people eat me it doesn't make any sound. That's because I'm soft."

"We are both fruits, we both taste nice and we are both healthy foods," said the apple and banana together.

19. Apple can be .... in colour

(a) red (b) green
(c) yellow (d) All of these

20. .... is soft and makes no sound when it is eaten.

(a) Apple
(b) Banana
(c) All of these
(d) None of the above

21. Find the antonym of 'hard' that is used in the passage.

(a) soft (b) crunchy
(c) nice (d) healthy

22. Choose the synonym of 'same' from the following options.

(a) different (b) nice
(c) similar (d) None of these

Passage 6

One day, King Akbar picked up a piece of chalk and drew a line on the floor.

"Birbal", he said to his friend, "I want you to make this line shorter. But you mustn't rub out the ends of the line."

Birbal looked at the line and thought. Then he drew a long line under King Akbar's line. "Look", said Birbal, "My line is longer than your line. So your line is shorter!"

King Akbar laughed, "You are right, Birbal," he said, "You made my line shorter. What a clever answer!"

23. What did Akbar do one day?

(a) Called his ministers
(b) Went out
(c) Drew a line with a chalk
(d) Sang music

24. What did he ask Birbal to do?

(a) Make the line bigger
(b) Make the line shorter
(c) Draw the line again
(d) Go away from the court

25. How did Birbal solve the problem?

(a) Went away without solving
(b) Drew a line
(c) Drew a longer line than Akbar's
(d) Refused to solve the problem

26. Write an antonym of the word 'clever'.

(a) Simpleton (b) Smart
(c) Foolish (d) Witty

Chapter 18

Communication Skills

Directions (Q. Nos. 1-21) Complete the following conversations and fill in the blanks by choosing the correct options.

1. Teacher: Which is your favourite subject?
Student: ....
(a) I love Maths.
(b) I don't like any subject.
(c) I don't need to tell you.
(d) Just go away

2. Ankit: Mother, I have finished my home work. May I go to Anju's house now?
Mother: No, ...
(a) You can (b) You cannot
(c) You could not (d) None of these

3. Mother: Shruti, you have got a very low score this time. ....
Shruti: Yes, Mom I will.
(a) You cannot work harder for the future
(b) You should not work hard in the future.
(c) you can work harder in the future
(d) You must work harder in the future.

4. Ruchi: .... but I can't dance equally well.
Shuchi: You should take guidance from Suraj Sir. He will tell you some tips.
(a) I can't sing well
(b) I can sing well
(c) I am singing well
(d) I am not singing well

5. Gaurav: Papa, can I go out and play?
Father: Sorry, ... because we have to go to the doctor today.
(a) You can go and play
(b) You cannot do so today
(c) You will not go today
(d) You should go and play

6. Megha: We are going to Kashmir this year.
Neha: Wow! ....
(a) Can I come with you?
(b) Can I come along?
(c) Can't I come along?
(d) Why will you not take me?

7. Simran: Have you bought a birthday gift for Pooja?
Kanak: Yes, but I don't know ....
(a) how to buy it.
(b) how to keep it a secret.
(c) how to pack it.
(d) how to throw it.

8. Amy: Mother, I have something to tell you.

Mother: ....

(a) What? (b) How it is?

(c) What is it? (d) Yes

9. Teacher: Ruhi, why didn't you come to school yesterday?

Ruhi: Madam, ...

(a) my mother was well

(b) my mother was not well

(c) my mother is good

(d) my mother cooked tasty food

10. Shopkeeper: What do you want, son?

Child: ....

(a) I want three packs of biscuit.

(b) I buy three packs of biscuit.

(c) I cannot buy three packs of biscuit.

(d) I shall buy three packs of biscuit.

11.

(a) Hello. I am Vishnu.

(b) Hey

(c) I will not talk to you

(d) Hello Raju

12.

(a) Hello, My name are Kunal

(b) Hey, My name was Kunal

(c) Hello, your name is not Bimal

(d) Hello, Bimal. I'm Kunal.

13.

(a) Hi, it's a bag.

(b) Hi, Sam! It's my tiffin box.

(c) Hi, Sam! I can't tell you.

(d) Hi, I'm going.

14.

(a) What is your hand in?

(b) What was in your hand?

(c) What's that in your hand?

(d) What's this in your hand?

15.

(a) It's a bag.

(b) It's green thing.

(c) It's a kit.

(d) It's a bottle.

16.

(a) These are not pens.
(b) These are colour pencils.
(c) These are erasers.
(d) These are rockets.

17.

(a) It's a cow. (b) It's a bull.
(c) It's a buffalo. (d) It's a dog.

18.

(a) I read magazines. (b) I read my books.
(c) I exercise. (d) I sleep.

19.

(a) He is reading newspaper.
(b) He reads newspaper.
(c) He read newspaper.
(d) He will read newspaper.

20.

(a) Please go away.
(b) I am not good. Thank you.
(c) You are not looking good. Bye.
(d) I'm good. Thank you.

21.

(a) I'm from Kanpur, how about you?
(b) I'm from Kanpur and you?
(c) I was from Kanpur, and you?
(d) I will be from Kanpur, and you?

22. What would you say when you want to make a request?

(a) Sorry (b) Thank you
(c) Please (d) It's okay

23. What would you say if you want to leave a conversation in between?

(a) Help me!
(b) Thanks a lot
(c) Bye
(d) Excuse me

24. When you make a mistake, what do you say to apologize?
(a) It happens
(b) Sorry
(c) I am happy to do that
(d) Please

25. When you wake up in the morning, how do you wish your family members?
(a) Good night (b) Good afternoon
(c) Good morning (d) Good evening

26. When you meet someone for the first time, how do you greet them?
(a) Hello (b) Bye
(c) Excuse me (d) Go away

27. What do you say before going to bed?
(a) Good evening (b) Bye, I am going
(c) I am sleeping (d) Good night

28. What would you say when someone helps you or gives you a present or a compliment?
(a) Nice to meet you (b) Nice
(c) Thank you (d) See you

29. When someone goes for a long journey, how do you wish them?
(a) Bye
(b) See you after a while
(c) Have a happy and safe journey
(d) I want to go with you

30. What do you say to encourage your friend before an exam?
(a) I am with you
(b) Let's go
(c) Okay
(d) All the best

31. You want to go to an amusement park with your parents but they are not taking you. How would you make a request in such a situation?
(a) Mummy, I will go to the amusement park.
(b) Mummy, I am going to the amusement park myself.
(c) Mummy, please take me to the park.
(d) Mummy, I will not talk to you.

32. Choose the correct response.
Aunt: Wow, son! Your handwriting is very beautiful.
(a) I want a present.
(b) Thank you, aunt.
(c) I am happy to see you.
(d) I want to go with you.

33. A flower vase has been broken by you. You would apologize to your mom by saying
(a) Sorry, mummy. I will be more careful next time.
(b) Mummy, I have not done it.
(c) I will fix it, don't worry
(d) You should buy a new one.

34. Your friend has brought your favourite toy as your birthday gift. You would thank her by saying
(a) Thank you. I am happy.
(b) Thank you, it's nice.
(c) Thank a lot.
(d) Thanks a lot. This is the best toy I have received today.

35. You came across a stranger in your street who is trying to talk to you. Choose the correct response for the given situation.
Stranger: Hello, child, Where do you live?
(a) I live in the 5th house counting from here.
(b) I'm sorry, I am not allowed to talk to strangers.
(c) I will call police.
(d) I am going, bye.

PRACTICE SET 01

1. Choose the correct predicate to complete the sentence. We ....
   (a) am going to play football.
   (b) is going to play football.
   (c) was going to play football.
   (d) are going to play football.

2. What is the plural form of the word 'Thief'?
   (a) Thiefs (b) Thieves
   (c) Thievs (d) Thefs

3. Use the correct pronoun for the noun given in the bracket.
   Delhi is a big city. (Delhi) .... is also the capital of our country.
   (a) That (b) He (c) It (d) She

4. Complete the sentence with a suitable verb. A tailor .... clothes.
   (a) stretches (b) stitches
   (c) stitching (d) stitch

5. Answer the following question with the correct use of tense.
   What do you do in school?
   I .... in school.
   (a) read and play
   (b) reading and playing
   (c) reads and plays
   (d) read and playing

6. Fill in the blank using appropriate articles.
   .... Ganga is the name of .... river in India.
   (a) A, a (b) The, the
   (c) The, a (d) The, an

7. Find the adjectives from the following sentence.
   He is tall, dark and handsome.
   (a) tall
   (b) tall, dark
   (c) dark
   (d) tall, dark, handsome

8. Fill in the blank by choosing the appropriate adverb from the options.
   He wrote the exam ....
   (a) neat (b) nice
   (c) neatly (d) neater

9. Fill in the blank by choosing the appropriate conjunction from the options.
   The paper was lengthy .... she finished it before time.
   (a) but (b) and (c) or (d) yet

10. Find the preposition from the options.
    (a) Smartly (b) But
    (c) Through (d) It

11. Which of the following sentences is properly punctuated?
    (a) Ram, Charu, Mehtab and Ravi are in the same class.
    (b) Ram; Charu; Mehtab and Ravi are in the same class
    (c) Ram Charu Methtab and, Ravi are in the same class,
    (d) Ram, Charu, mehtab and ravi are in the same class.

12. Choose the correct sentence from the following options.
(a) Would you like coffee but tea?
(b) Would you like coffee and tea?
(c) Would you like coffee or tea?
(d) Would you like coffee so tea?

13. Unjumble the following letters to make a meaningful word.
LPYATR
(a) Partyl (b) Pratly (c) Partly (d) Pralyt

14. Unjumble the following to make a meaningful sentence.
he/was/cricket/started/3 years/ Sachin/old/when/playing
(a) Sachin playing cricket when started was 3 years old.
(b) Sachin playing started cricket when he was 3 years old.
(c) Sachin started cricket playing when he was 3 years old.
(d) Sachin started playing cricket when he was 3 years old.

15. Find the odd one out.
(a) Flock (b) Herd (c) Swarm (d) Break

16. Match the words given in List A with their opposites given in List B.

	List A		List B
A.	Full	1.	Dumb
B.	Right	2.	Unfair
C.	Fair	3.	Empty
D.	Smart	4.	Wrong

Codes

	A	B	C	D		A	B	C	D
(a)	3	2	4	1	(b)	3	4	2	1
(c)	3	4	1	2	(d)	4	3	2	1

17. Find the conjunction in the following sentence.
Roshan called me while he was travelling in the Metro.
(a) in (b) me
(c) while (d) travelling

18. 'Smart' is ....
(a) a verb (b) a noun
(c) an adjective (d) an article

19. Fill in the blank using appropriate article.
Yami is .... actress.
(a) a (b) an (c) the (d) a or the

20. Find the common noun from the following.
(a) Yami Gautam
(b) Sardar Patel Street
(c) Kamani Auditorium
(d) Class

Directions (Q. Nos. 21-22) Complete the following conversations.

21. Rohit : Mumma, I'm very hungry. Can we have the dinner please?
Mother: Dinner's ready. ....
(a) Rohit, please lie the table
(b) Rohit, please lie down the table
(c) Rohit, please lay the table
(d) Rohit, please lay down the table

22. Kiran: .... ?
Rajat: I don't have any special plans.
(a) What are you doing this weekend?
(b) What were you doing this weekend?
(c) What have you doing this weekend?
(d) What will you doing that weekend?

23. Fill in the blank using appropriate preposition.

Delhi is .... Mumbai and Jammu.

(a) in (b) under
(c) between (d) over

24. Fill in the blank with the opposite of the word given in bracket.

Rashi is a .... (brave) girl.

(a) timid (b) unbrave
(c) clever (d) frightened

25. Find the correctly punctuated sentence from the following.

(a) have you been to Jaipur.
(b) Have you been to Jaipur.
(c) have you been to Jaipur?
(d) Have you been to Jaipur?

26. Find the noun/s in the following sentence.

Many people own a smartphone these days.

(a) people
(b) people, smartphone
(c) smartphone
(d) people, smartphone, days

27. Choose the correct similar meaning word for the following word.
Happy

(a) Gay (b) Joy
(c) Smile (d) Day

28. Arrange the following letters to make a meaningful word.

OTRTOEIS

(a) Trotoise (b) Tortoise
(c) Testorio (d) Troiseto

29. Choose the wrongly spelt word.

(a) Certain (b) Criteria
(c) Scisors (d) Application

30. Choose the correct pair of words.

(a) Bacon for eggs (b) Back and forth
(c) By to large (d) Bits or pieces

Directions (Q. Nos. 31-35) Read the passage given below and answer the questions that follow.

Robin went to the library. He wanted to read a story book. There were many small children in the library. They were reading books. Robin took a story book and started reading it. It had many colourful pictures. He wanted to read all the stories but the librarian told him to leave as the library was going to be closed for the day.

31. Where did Robin go?

(a) To school (b) To play
(c) To library (d) To the mall

32. There were .... small children in the ....

(a) many, school (b) many, library
(c) more, school (d) more, library

33. The word 'It' in the passage is used for

(a) librarian (b) library
(c) Robin (d) story book

34. The opposite of the word 'small' is

(a) tiny (b) beg (c) big (d) bigger

35. Find the adjective in the following sentence from the passage.

There were many small children in the library.

(a) many (b) children
(c) the (d) small

PRACTICE SET 02

1. Choose the predicate of the given sentence. Sakshi is a good girl.
(a) Sakshi is (b) is a good girl
(c) a good girl (d) good girl

2. Select the countable noun from the following.
(a) Sugar (b) Salt
(c) Milk shake (d) Pony

3. Count the number of pronouns in the following.
Kamal is in Class II. He is hard of hearing. His father took him to a doctor. The doctor gave a machine to Kamal. After using it, he was able to hear properly.
(a) 2 (b) 3 (c) 1 (d) 4

4. Find the verbs in the following line.
Rahul studies and plays well.
(a) studies
(b) plays
(c) Both (a) and (b)
(d) Neither (a) nor (b)

5. Fill in the blank by using the correct form of tense.
The Sun .... in the West.
(a) setted (b) sets
(c) will set (d) will be setting

6. Choose the sentence in which the articles are used properly.
(a) I went to an hotel today.
(b) Karan is an honest man.
(c) I had the banana in breakfast.
(d) A apple a day keeps doctor away.

7. Choose the adjective from the following.
(a) Close (b) Closely
(c) Closed (d) Closet

8. Find the adverb in the following sentence.
Abraham is a very smart boy.
(a) smart (b) boy
(c) is (d) very

9. Which of the following is not a conjunction?
(a) And (b) But
(c) While (d) Between

10. Fill in the blank using appropriate preposition.
The train went .... the tunnel.
(a) through (b) on
(c) between (d) across

11. Fill in the blank by choosing the correct option.
The .... was shining.........
(a) sun, Brightly
(b) Sun, Brightly
(c) Sun, brightly
(d) sun, brightly

12. Choose the correct spelling.
(a) Laibrery (b) Librari
(c) Librery (d) Library

13. What word do you get by rearranging the letters PRPUEL?
(a) Prepul (b) Perpul
(c) Purple (d) Pulper

14. Rearrange the following to make a meaningful sentence.
gets / Sohini / easily / angry / very
(a) Sohini gets easily very angry.
(b) Sohini angry gets very easily.
(c) Sohini gets very easily angry.
(d) Sohini gets angry very easily.

15. Choose the odd one out from the following.
(a) Delhi (b) Suman
(c) Dotted (d) Pastry

16. Choose the opposite of the underlined word.
This is a <u>common</u> disease among children.
(a) decommon
(b) uncommon
(c) complex
(d) simple

17. A group of bees is called a
(a) swarm (b) herd
(c) flock (d) bunch

18. Which of the following is a proper noun?
(a) Cricketer
(b) Athelete
(c) Sportsperson
(d) Mahendra Singh Dhoni

19. What is the plural of Sea?
(a) Sea (b) Seas
(c) Sees (d) See

20. Which of the following sentences is punctuated properly?
(a) Shahid got married to mira.
(b) Shahid, got married to Mira.
(c) Shahid got married to mira.
(d) Shahid got married to Mira.

Directions (Q. Nos. 21 and 22) Complete the following conversations.

21. Ravi: Hi Karan, how're you doing?
Karan: .... ?
(a) Fine, and you?
(b) Fine, thank you. And you?
(c) I' m fine, okay.
(d) Okay.

22. Rita: Hello, Gita! I'm so pleased to meet you!
Gita: ....
(a) I'm so glad to meet you too!
(b) I' m so glad to meet you.
(c) I' m glad to meet you?
(d) Please go!

23. Choose the correctly punctuated sentence.
(a) papa has invited some friends for dinner
(b) Papa has invited, some friends for dinner
(c) papa has invited some friends for dinner
(d) Papa has invited some friends for dinner.

24. Complete the word pair.
Salt and ....
(a) Sugar (b) Cream
(c) Pepper (d) Table

25. What is the masculine of vixen?
(a) Tiger (b) Fox
(c) Wolf (d) Hyena

26. What is the feminine of waiter?
(a) Manager
(b) Waitress
(c) Waiterlady
(d) Waiterwoman

27. Fill in the blank with correct option.
What .... you want me to do?
(a) do (b) is
(c) am (d) are

28. Choose the word similar in meaning to the word 'crack'.
(a) Sharp (b) Dull
(c) Break (d) Piece

29. Complete the word pair.
Bread and ....
(a) Fork (b) Spoon
(c) Sauce (d) Butter

30. Choose the word which is similar in meaning to 'Large'
(a) Enormous
(b) Short
(c) High
(d) Thin

Directions (Q. Nos. 31-35) Read the passage given below and answer the questions that follows.

Kanishk has an exam tomorrow. He is studying for the exam now. His parents are in the office and his grandfather is looking after him. He is an obedient child. His younger brother is also at home. His name is Karan. Karan is too small to go to school. So, he stays at home when his brother goes to school.

31. What does Kanishk has tomorrow?
(a) Exam (b) Match
(c) Party (d) Exhibition

32. Kanishk's parents are ....
(a) at home (b) in the mall
(c) at the office (d) in a party

33. Find an adjective in the following sentence.
He is an obedient child.
(a) child (b) an
(c) He (d) obedient

34. The opposite of the word 'younger' is
(a) older (b) elder
(c) eldest (d) oldest

35. The word 'too' in the passage means
(a) near (b) less (c) very (d) more

ANSWERS

Chapter 1 Nouns

1. (c)	2. (b)	3. (d)	4. (c)	5. (d)	6. (a)	7. (b)	8. (d)	9. (a)	10. (c)
11. (b)	12. (d)	13. (a)	14. (b)	15. (c)	16. (a)	17. (a)	18. (b)	19. (d)	20. (b)
21. (b)	22. (d)	23. (b)	24. (a)	25. (a)	26. (b)	27. (c)	28. (a)	29. (c)	30. (a)
31. (b)	32. (a)	33. (c)	34. (b)	35. (c)	36. (c)				

Chapter 2 Pronouns

1. (b)	2. (c)	3. (d)	4. (a)	5. (c)	6. (c)	7. (b)	8. (b)	9. (c)	10. (a)
11. (d)	12. (b)	13. (c)	14. (b)	15. (b)	16. (b)	17. (b)	18. (c)	19. (a)	20. (a)
21. (b)	22. (b)	23. (c)	24. (b)	25. (b)	26. (a)	27. (b)	28. (c)	29. (d)	30. (c)

Chapter 3 Verbs

1. (c)	2. (a)	3. (b)	4. (b)	5. (b)	6. (c)	7. (b)	8. (a)	9. (d)	10. (a)
11. (c)	12. (b)	13. (a)	14. (d)	15. (a)	16. (c)	17. (b)	18. (a)	19. (c)	20. (b)
21. (a)	22. (b)	23. (b)	24. (b)	25. (c)	26. (a)	27. (c)	28. (c)	29. (b)	30. (a)

Chapter 4 Adverbs

1. (c)	2. (d)	3. (b)	4. (b)	5. (b)	6. (d)	7. (b)	8. (c)	9. (d)	10. (c)
11. (b)	12. (c)	13. (c)	14. (d)	15. (b)	16. (b)	17. (b)	18. (c)	19. (a)	20. (b)
21. (b)	22. (b)	23. (c)	24. (b)	25. (a)	26. (a)				

Chapter 5 Adjectives

1. (b)	2. (a)	3. (d)	4. (c)	5. (a)	6. (b)	7. (c)	8. (d)	9. (b)	10. (d)
11. (b)	12. (a)	13. (b)	14. (c)	15. (c)	16. (b)	17. (c)	18. (a)	19. (b)	20. (c)
21. (d)	22. (d)	23. (c)	24. (a)	25. (b)	26. (a)	27. (c)	28. (d)	29. (b)	30. (c)

Chapter 6 Articles

1. (a)	2. (a)	3. (b)	4. (c)	5. (d)	6. (c)	7. (b)	8. (c)	9. (c)	10. (c)
11. (b)	12. (a)	13. (d)	14. (c)	15. (a)	16. (c)	17. (b)	18. (a)	19. (b)	20. (b)
21. (c)	22. (a)	23. (b)	24. (c)	25. (a)	26. (b)	27. (a)	28. (d)	29. (b)	30. (c)
31. (c)	32. (b)	33. (a)	34. (b)	35. (a)	36. (d)				

Chapter 7 Prepositions

1. (a)	2. (c)	3. (b)	4. (d)	5. (b)	6. (c)	7. (a)	8. (b)	9. (d)	10. (d)
11. (c)	12. (c)	13. (b)	14. (c)	15. (b)	16. (a)	17. (c)	18. (b)	19. (d)	20. (a)
21. (a)	22. (c)	23. (d)	24. (d)	25. (b)	26. (d)	27. (c)	28. (a)	29. (c)	30. (d)

Chapter 8 Conjunctions

1. (d)	**2.** (a)	**3.** (b)	**4.** (d)	**5.** (c)	**6.** (c)	**7.** (b)	**8.** (c)	**9.** (b)	**10.** (c)
11. (a)	**12.** (d)	**13.** (b)	**14.** (c)	**15.** (b)	**16.** (a)	**17.** (b)	**18.** (d)	**19.** (c)	**20.** (a)
21. (a)	**22.** (d)	**23.** (b)	**24.** (c)	**25.** (d)	**26.** (b)	**27.** (c)	**28.** (d)	**29.** (a)	**30.** (b)
31. (a)	**32.** (c)	**33.** (b)	**34.** (b)	**35.** (b)	**36.** (a)				

Chapter 9 Punctuations

1. (b)	**2.** (c)	**3.** (d)	**4.** (c)	**5.** (b)	**6.** (b)	**7.** (c)	**8.** (b)	**9.** (a)	**10.** (c)
11. (a)	**12.** (c)	**13.** (b)	**14.** (c)	**15.** (b)	**16.** (c)	**17.** (d)	**18.** (b)	**19.** (b)	**20.** (d)
21. (c)	**22.** (c)	**23.** (c)	**24.** (a)	**25.** (c)	**26.** (c)				

Chapter 10 Sentences

1. (a)	**2.** (c)	**3.** (c)	**4.** (b)	**5.** (d)	**6.** (c)	**7.** (b)	**8.** (a)	**9.** (d)	**10.** (b)
11. (b)	**12.** (b)	**13.** (c)	**14.** (c)	**15.** (c)	**16.** (c)	**17.** (a)	**18.** (b)	**19.** (a)	**20.** (c)
21. (c)	**22.** (a)	**23.** (c)	**24.** (a)	**25.** (d)					

Chapter 11 Simple Tenses

1. (a)	**2.** (d)	**3.** (c)	**4.** (b)	**5.** (c)	**6.** (c)	**7.** (b)	**8.** (b)	**9.** (c)	**10.** (c)
11. (d)	**12.** (a)	**13.** (c)	**14.** (c)	**15.** (a)	**16.** (c)	**17.** (c)	**18.** (c)	**19.** (c)	**20.** (b)
21. (b)	**22.** (a)	**23.** (c)	**24.** (b)	**25.** (c)	**26.** (b)	**27.** (c)	**28.** (a)	**29.** (c)	**30.** (b)
31. (b)	**32.** (b)	**33.** (c)	**34.** (b)	**35.** (c)	**36.** (b)	**37.** (a)	**38.** (b)	**39.** (d)	**40.** (c)

Chapter 12 Words and their Meanings

1. (b)	**2.** (c)	**3.** (b)	**4.** (d)	**5.** (c)	**6.** (a)	**7.** (c)	**8.** (c)	**9.** (b)	**10.** (c)
11. (d)	**12.** (c)	**13.** (a)	**14.** (b)	**15.** (c)	**16.** (d)	**17.** (a)	**18.** (c)	**19.** (b)	**20.** (c)
21. (b)	**22.** (c)	**23.** (a)	**24.** (d)	**25.** (a)					

Chapter 13 Words and their Opposites

1. (b)	**2.** (d)	**3.** (b)	**4.** (a)	**5.** (c)	**6.** (d)	**7.** (a)	**8.** (b)	**9.** (c)	**10.** (b)
11. (c)	**12.** (c)	**13.** (b)	**14.** (c)	**15.** (b)	**16.** (c)	**17.** (b)	**18.** (d)	**19.** (c)	**20.** (a)
21. (c)	**22.** (a)	**23.** (d)	**24.** (b)	**25.** (c)					

Chapter 14 Spelling Test

1. (b)	**2.** (c)	**3.** (d)	**4.** (c)	**5.** (b)	**6.** (c)	**7.** (c)	**8.** (c)	**9.** (b)	**10.** (d)
11. (c)	**12.** (d)	**13.** (b)	**14.** (d)	**15.** (b)	**16.** (c)	**17.** (b)	**18.** (a)	**19.** (c)	**20.** (d)
21. (d)	**22.** (b)	**23.** (c)	**24.** (d)	**25.** (c)	**26.** (d)	**27.** (a)	**28.** (c)	**29.** (d)	**30.** (a)
31. (b)	**32.** (c)								

Chapter 15 Word Pair and Odd One Out

1. (a)	**2.** (b)	**3.** (b)	**4.** (c)	**5.** (d)	**6.** (a)	**7.** (b)	**8.** (d)	**9.** (c)	**10.** (b)
11. (d)	**12.** (c)	**13.** (b)	**14.** (a)	**15.** (b)	**16.** (d)	**17.** (b)	**18.** (d)	**19.** (b)	**20.** (a)
21. (d)	**22.** (c)	**23.** (d)	**24.** (b)	**25.** (d)	**26.** (b)	**27.** (b)	**28.** (b)	**29.** (c)	**30.** (b)
31. (c)	**32.** (c)	**33.** (d)	**34.** (d)						

Chapter 16 Spelling Test

1. (d)	**2.** (a)	**3.** (b)	**4.** (c)	**5.** (b)	**6.** (a)	**7.** (b)	**8.** (c)	**9.** (a)	**10.** (b)
11. (b)	**12.** (c)	**13.** (d)	**14.** (c)	**15.** (a)	**16.** (b)	**17.** (a)	**18.** (b)	**19.** (c)	**20.** (d)
21. (b)	**22.** (a)	**23.** (c)	**24.** (d)	**25.** (b)	**26.** (d)	**27.** (c)	**28.** (a)	**29.** (c)	**30.** (d)
31. (c)	**32.** (d)	**33.** (b)	**34.** (a)	**35.** (b)	**36.** (c)	**37.** (d)	**38.** (c)	**39.** (b)	**40.** (a)

Chapter 17 Reading Comprehension

1. (c)	**2.** (a)	**3.** (b)	**4.** (d)	**5.** (d)	**6.** (b)	**7.** (d)	**8.** (c)	**9.** (d)	**10.** (a)
11. (a)	**12.** (c)	**13.** (a)	**14.** (c)	**15.** (d)	**16.** (b)	**17.** (a)	**18.** (c)	**19.** (d)	**20.** (b)
21. (a)	**22.** (c)	**23.** (c)	**24.** (b)	**25.** (c)	**26.** (c)				

Chapter 18 Communication Skills

1. (a)	**2.** (b)	**3.** (d)	**4.** (b)	**5.** (b)	**6.** (b)	**7.** (c)	**8.** (c)	**9.** (b)	**10.** (a)
11. (a)	**12.** (d)	**13.** (b)	**14.** (c)	**15.** (a)	**16.** (b)	**17.** (c)	**18.** (b)	**19.** (b)	**20.** (d)
21. (b)	**22.** (c)	**23.** (d)	**24.** (b)	**25.** (c)	**26.** (a)	**27.** (d)	**28.** (c)	**29.** (c)	**30.** (d)
31. (c)	**32.** (b)	**33.** (a)	**34.** (d)	**35.** (b)					

Practice Set 1

1. (d)	**2.** (b)	**3.** (c)	**4.** (b)	**5.** (a)	**6.** (c)	**7.** (d)	**8.** (c)	**9.** (a)	**10.** (c)
11. (a)	**12.** (c)	**13.** (c)	**14.** (d)	**15.** (d)	**16.** (b)	**17.** (c)	**18.** (c)	**19.** (b)	**20.** (d)
21. (c)	**22.** (a)	**23.** (c)	**24.** (a)	**25.** (d)	**26.** (d)	**27.** (a)	**28.** (b)	**29.** (c)	**30.** (b)
31. (c)	**32.** (b)	**33.** (d)	**34.** (c)	**35.** (d)					

Practice Set 2

1. (b)	**2.** (d)	**3.** (d)	**4.** (c)	**5.** (b)	**6.** (b)	**7.** (c)	**8.** (d)	**9.** (d)	**10.** (a)
11. (c)	**12.** (d)	**13.** (c)	**14.** (d)	**15.** (c)	**16.** (b)	**17.** (a)	**18.** (d)	**19.** (b)	**20.** (d)
21. (b)	**22.** (a)	**23.** (d)	**24.** (c)	**25.** (b)	**26.** (b)	**27.** (a)	**28.** (c)	**29.** (d)	**30.** (a)
31. (a)	**32.** (c)	**33.** (d)	**34.** (b)	**35.** (c)					